July 23, 2011 – State Game Lodge
Custer State Park,
South Dakota

✓ = we've
seen/been there

Wood Lily

Custer State Park

From the Mountains to the Plains

Photography by

Paul Horsted

Design by Camille Riner

Golden Valley Press

How many loving clouds will fold
The piny peaks in tender mist ....

Badger Clark

Custer State Park *From the Mountains to the Plains*

Published by Golden Valley Press, an imprint of Dakota Photographic LLC, 24905 Mica Ridge Road, Custer, S.D., 57730.

Edited by Dorothea Edgington.

Poetry excerpts in this book are by Badger Clark, from the book **Sky Lines and Wood Smoke**, ©Jessie Y. Sundstrom (Jessie Y. Sundstrom, Custer, S.D., 1984), used with permission. The excerpts appearing on pages 3, 12 and 95 are from the poem *I Must Come Back*; page 44 is from *Deer Trails*; page 58 is from *God Meets Me in the Mountains*; page 80 is from *Myself and I*. For more about the life and work of Badger Clark, see the book **Badger Clark, Cowboy Poet With Universal Appeal**, by Jessie Y. Sundstrom (Jessie Y. Sundstrom, Custer, S.D., 2004). Available from the Badger Clark Memorial Society, Box 351, Custer, S.D., 57730.

For more information about Custer State Park, contact the Park Headquarters at (605) 255-4515, or write Custer State Park, HC 83 Box 70, Custer, S.D., 57730, or visit www.custerstatepark.info.

All landscape photos in this book were taken within Custer State Park or looking into the Park from nearby Harney Peak. Some wildlife and plant specimens shown in this book were photographed outside Park boundaries in similar Black Hills habitat.

Created, produced, and designed in the United States of America. Printed in Korea.

First Edition: September, 2004.

ISBN number: 0-9718053-2-6

Library of Congress Control Number: 2004109071

Custer State Park
From the Mountains to the Plains

Contents

Introduction

Custer State Park is perhaps the most diverse state park in the country. As one of the largest state parks at more than 71,000 acres, its natural scenery and rich cultural history rival any national treasure. From its towering granite outcroppings to its rolling mixed-grass prairie, from its historical sites to its rustic mountain resorts, Custer State Park is truly a reservoir of natural and cultural resources.

The story of Custer State Park begins in 1912 with a progressive conservationist and politician named Peter Norbeck. South Dakota Governor, later United States Senator, Norbeck crafted a deal which allowed school holding lands to be consolidated into a nearly 48,000-acre tract named Custer State Forest. He envisioned a landmass offering a mixture of habitat for a variety of songbirds, birds of prey, reptiles, and amphibians. His plan also provided for a sanctuary, Custer State Game Preserve, where wildlife such as bison, elk, bighorn sheep and mountain goats could thrive. Even in its infancy, it was apparent to Norbeck that this "park-like" area was a special place, promising to attract national attention forever. Hence, in 1919, Norbeck instigated the name change to Custer State Park. In later years, with the addition of the adjoining Sylvan Lake and Stockade Lake areas, the park continued its preservation of treasured resources.

South Dakota without Custer State Park is unimaginable. It was the first state park in South Dakota, and it is often referred to as the "crown jewel of the state park system." Every park has its own story with plots, characters, and great endings; however, Custer State Park exhibits an unmatched uniqueness: its stories never end. With more than 1.8 million visitors each year, Norbeck's dream for South Dakota has been accomplished. Custer State Park provides the state and nation with the preservation of natural wonders and awe-inspiring history, and it has become a sanctuary favored by thousands of its guests.

Bradley Block
Chief of Interpretation, Custer State Park

Preface

I Feel Blessed to have known and photographed Custer State Park for nearly two decades. Although I still feel like we're getting acquainted (71,000 acres is a lot to know!), I've come to love this landscape which stretches from the foot of the eastern Black Hills to the towering granite ranges of the Needles. It seems that nearly every visit turns to adventure: I've chased rainbows across the prairie, wandered with the bison herd along the Wildlife Loop Road, hiked to Little Devil's Tower at sunset, and watched lightning play over Sylvan Lake. All of these events are represented in the following pages.

My heartfelt thanks are due the following people for their assistance, suggestions and support: The staff of Custer State Park, especially Bradley Block, Craig Pugsley, and Rollie Noem; Steve Baldwin, Black Hills Parks and Forests Association; Phil Lampert and Wade Lampert, Custer State Park Resort Company; and Jessie Y. Sundstrom, author and historian. Thanks also to Dorothea Edgington for copy editing; to several other dear friends for their final review of the text; to Governor and Senator Peter Norbeck for his foresight in setting aside this beautiful area starting in 1919; and to Badger Clark for his poetry about the Park and the Black Hills. Badger says so much in so few words, and his work provides the perfect accent for the photographs here.

The images in this book include my best work, some of it from more than a decade ago, much of it from more recent years when my wife, Camille, daughter, Anna Marie, and I have lived near the town of Custer, our adopted home. The beauty and serenity of Custer State Park and the Black Hills called us to come here from elsewhere in South Dakota. Camille and Anna, I could not have done this book without you!

Special thanks also to Burt and Gladys Horsted and to Al and Linda Riner for their love and encouragement all these years.

I hope the photographs shown in these pages will do justice to the tremendous beauty and variety that God and nature have bestowed here. My intent with this book is not to create a guide to every plant and animal, nor to show everything you can see or do here. My wish is merely to share my favorite images in hope they might encourage you to start, or continue, or perhaps remember with fondness your own exploration of this special place, "From the Mountains to the Plains ...."

Whether with camera or only in your mind's eye, enjoy the moment and the time you have here.

Paul Horsted
Custer, S.D.
June, 2004

Opposite page: With dinner ready for his young, a male mountain bluebird pauses near his nest. Watch for these colorful birds who "carry the sky on their backs" along the Wildlife Loop Road and other prairie areas of Custer State Park.

Inset photo courtesy Custer State Park.

Badger Clark was South Dakota's first Poet Laureate. Living simply in a cabin built with his own hands and aptly named "The Badger Hole," he pondered the solitude and beauty of Custer State Park. He then penned the lines which appear in part on the pages opening each section of this book. The quotes are from one of Badger's books, **Sky Lines and Wood Smoke,** first published in 1935.

During the summer season, you can visit The Badger Hole and see it as it was left upon Badger Clark's death in 1957. Tucked away over the hill from Legion Lake, it provides a glimpse into a simpler time and way of life.

The photo composite (above) shows Badger's cabin and a portrait (inset) from later years as he shared his poetry at one of his many public appearances.

Opposite page: In Badger Clark's bedroom, an American flag hangs behind the bed and his trademark dress boots stand ready at the bed's foot. A patriot, Badger had an American flag represented in every room of his cabin.

Plains

*What sunsets turn the sky to gold
And distant plains to amethyst ....*

Badger Clark

Purple coneflowers (above) flourish on Custer State Park's eastern mid-summer prairie.

Previous spread: A line of bison (left), commonly known as buffalo, trail across the brown fall prairie under a waning moon. Insulated against cold and snow in a thick winter coat, bison (right) roam Custer State Park.

Opposite page: A grasshopper poses atop a purple coneflower.

Following spread: As darkness descends, a few stars twinkle above the forest skyline along the Wildlife Loop Road. The Big Dipper constellation is visible at right.

A spider prepares for night, and for dinner, by spinning a web at sunset.

Opposite page: A Gray Hairstreak butterfly searches for nectar on a woolly verbena flower.

A pronghorn kid (above) nuzzles its mother. Pronghorns are generally referred to as antelope.

Opposite page: Prairie dogs go about their business at their "town" along the southern end of the Wildlife Loop.

Following spread: A rainbow spills from sky to prairie on the Park's eastern edge.

Swishing his tail, a bull bison strides over a hilltop and across a golden sunrise.

Opposite page: Her woolly hair adorned with burrs, a young cow chews her cud in morning sunshine.

A young bison calf shows his agility by scratching his nose with a hind hoof.

Opposite page: A prickly pear cactus blooms in vibrant yellows in early July.

A bumblebee (above) probes a Flodman's thistle for nectar.

Opposite page: Caught in mid-bray, one of the infamous "begging burros" performs along the Wildlife Loop Road.

Following spread: Pronghorns graze a ridgeline at the first light of dawn.

A time exposure of six hours (top) captures stars wheeling across the night sky above a lone pine tree; an airplane's lights cut across nature's pattern. Summer and winter follow each other (bottom, left and right) in an enduring cycle as seconds, days, and seasons flow past this same tree in Custer State Park.

Opposite page: A prairie rose, beautiful to behold, is merely lunch to a small grasshopper.

A pronghorn antelope buck (above) closely crops his favorite prairie grasses.

Opposite page: Western wallflowers adorn a prairie which seems to stretch to infinity on the Park's eastern edge.

Following spread: Custer State Park's bison herd, one of the largest in the country, wanders across thousands of acres of prairie and forest.

Choosing a lofty perch on a prairie boulder (above), an upland sandpiper chortles its mating call.

Opposite page: The sego lily is one of a multitude of showy flowers easily found on the summer prairie.

A pronghorn antelope buck surveys his domain in the southeastern portion of the Park.

Opposite page: A bison calf stays close to mother as the herd moves to greener springtime pastures. Calves are usually cinnamon colored at birth, gradually changing to a darker brown as they mature.

A highlight of the fall season, the buffalo roundup is an opportunity to see 1,500 animals moving across the prairie, at times guided by cowboys and wranglers in trucks and on horseback, at other times going where they will.

Opposite page: Few baby animals are more cute, or more curious, than a bison calf.

Water

*Wry as a streamlet's trickle
And wayward as my heart ....*

Badger Clark

Sylvan Lake (above) looks beautifully foreboding under an advancing storm.

Previous pages: The largest lake in the Park, Stockade Lake, (left) glows at sunset under a clearing storm. A fern accents a small waterfall (right) in Sunday Gulch below Sylvan Lake.

Opposite page: A redwing blackbird watches over his territory, a stretch of cattails along the shore of Stockade Lake.

Following spread: A large bison bull wanders along French Creek near the Horse Camp.

Sylvan Lake is an idyllic place for a family to relax and admire the view while fishing.

Opposite page: Willows frame a fog-enshrouded Legion Lake.

Rising fog (above) slowly reveals a bison resting on a distant ridge off the Wildlife Loop Road.

Opposite page: Bison amble across French Creek, pausing for a drink.

Following spread: Lightning bolts split the night sky above Sylvan Lake in a mid-summer storm. Raindrops on the camera lens create a swirl in the sky.

Hoarfrost decorates an oak leaf on a frigid winter morning.

Opposite page: A small waterfall glides over water-worn rocks in the French Creek Natural Area.

Mountains

*Where pines reach up the mountains
and the mountains up the blue ....*

Badger Clark

Harney Peak (above), seen in an aerial view, is the highest point in the Black Hills and a popular hiking destination. Several trails lead from Custer State Park to Harney's summit in the adjacent Black Elk Wilderness Area.

Previous spread: A daring rock climber (left) scales the Needle's Eye. The majestic Cathedral Spires (right) jut skyward through encircling mists.

Opposite page: Black-eyed Susans and purple beebalm, also called horsemint, surround an ancient tree stump.

A bighorn sheep ewe (above) munches on clover along the Wildlife Loop Road.

Opposite page: A cluster of tiny ladybugs gathers to mate at the summit of Mt. Coolidge. These little beetles may at times be seen in groups like this on Harney and other peaks in the Black Hills.

Following spread: Lightning curls across the sky over Custer State Park, seen here from the summit of Harney Peak. The Cathedral Spires are at lower right, with tower lights on Mt. Coolidge visible at left.

A delicate wildflower (above), the bracted spiderwort's purple hues delight the eye in June and July.

Opposite page: Ears alert, a mule deer rests while others stand watchfully nearby.

Following spread: A rainbow arcs over Sylvan Lake and the Harney Peak Range, seen from near Sylvan Lake Lodge after an afternoon thunderstorm.

Mountain goats (above three photos) are wild animals but seem to share human-like facial traits of wisdom, sleepiness, or good humor.

Opposite page: A bighorn sheep ram poses majestically as he pauses from browsing on birch leaves along the Black Hills Playhouse road.

Following spread: Granite peaks and forested ridges of the Needles area seem to rise from a primeval mist, conjuring a glimpse of the Black Hills as they may have appeared eons ago.

Against a backdrop of the Harney Peak Range, fresh snow decorates the forest near Stockade Lake.

Opposite page: Frigid winter mornings leave a frosty coat on pine cones and needles.

Fire is as natural as rain, wind or sunshine to the forests
and prairies of the Black Hills. Periodic fires help clear
downed timber and overgrowth of Ponderosa pine trees,
releasing minerals back to the soil and rejuvenating the
landscape. Planned, prescribed burns (such as this one in
the Park's southeastern corner) also help reduce the risk of
large, uncontrolled wildfires.

Two seasons after a wildfire, the formerly blackened landscape is ablaze with new growth on the upper slope of Mt. Coolidge.

Following spread: A magnificent bull elk parades across the dawn, with antlers held high.

People

*Let me get out in the hills again,
l and myself alone ....*

Badger Clark

A fly fisherman (above) tries his luck trout fishing at Sylvan Lake.

Previous spread: The photographer's shadow (left) chases across rock formations on Little Devil's Tower as sunlight plays across the Cathedral Spires. Two hikers (right) admire the view from Harney Peak into Custer State Park.

Opposite page: Trail riders cross French Creek near Horse Camp on a beautiful summer day.

Following spread: A climber finds solitude in the granite spires along the Needles Highway.

Bighorn sheep and visitors (above) have a close encounter along the Wildlife Loop Road.

Opposite page: The fire tower at Mt. Coolidge provides a panorama of the Black Hills and eastern plains. From here, Mt. Rushmore and Crazy Horse Memorial may be glimpsed in the distance.

Following spread: Fall colors decorate the landscape along the Needles Highway.

Each of the four lodges spread throughout Custer State Park is unique in its own way. All are open to the public for meals, lodging, or just soaking up the atmosphere. Sylvan Lake Resort (top) is located in one of the most scenic areas of the Park. Legion Lake Resort (bottom) is especially attractive to families.

Blue Bell Lodge and Resort (top) is a hideaway with a western touch, while the State Game Lodge (bottom) served as the Summer White House for President Calvin Coolidge in 1927. Bison often graze on the front lawn.

The Peter Norbeck Visitor Center (top), built in 1937 by the Civilian Conservation Corps, serves visitors to the park today as it has for decades. It is named for the South Dakota Governor (later Senator) who helped establish Custer State Park in 1919. The Wildlife Station Visitor Center (bottom, left), also built in 1937, originally served as a residence for the herdsman who tended the buffalo herd. The Black Hills Playhouse (bottom, right) has provided live summer theater to audiences since 1946.

A park interpreter (top, left) is framed in a cabin doorway at Gordon Stockade near the west side of the Park. The original Stockade was built in January, 1875 by the first gold seekers to follow Custer's Expedition of the previous summer. The overlook at Heddy Draw (top, right), presents a dramatic panorama of an area burned by forest fire in 1988. An evening campfire (bottom) at a Stockade Lake campground warms the body and soul in cool mountain air.

Following spread: The idyllic Black Hills view from above the "Honeymoon Cabin" near Sylvan Lake Lodge is eloquently described by the words of poet Badger Clark.

My Earth, the loveliness of you,
From all your gorgeous zodiac,
Down to a glistening drop of dew.
I must come back! I must come back!

Badger Clark

Above the clouds on Little Devil's Tower.

Photo: Camille Riner

About the Photographer

Paul Horsted has been taking photographs professionally for 25 years. He has worked as a staff photographer at the Sioux Falls (S.D.) *Argus Leader*, as chief photographer at South Dakota Tourism, and for the past 15 years as a freelance commercial photographer. His work has appeared in dozens of books and national magazines.

Paul's most significant project prior to this book was re-photographing photo sites of the Black Hills Expedition, where the first photos of the Black Hills were taken in 1874 as Gen. George Armstrong Custer explored the area. The resulting "then and now" images can be seen in the book **Exploring With Custer: The 1874 Black Hills Expedition,** published by Golden Valley Press.

Paul resides near Custer with his wife (the designer of this book), Camille Riner, and their daughter, Anna Marie.

Paul may be contacted through his web site, www.dakotaphoto.com.